The Wisdom Of Wilting

Collection of Poems

Shifa Thakkar

India | USA | UK

Copyright © Shifa Thakkar
All Rights Reserved.

This book has been self-published with all reasonable efforts taken to make the material error-free by the author. No part of this book shall be used, reproduced in any manner whatsoever without written permission from the author, except in the case of brief quotations embodied in critical articles and reviews.

The Author of this book is solely responsible and liable for its content including but not limited to the views, representations, descriptions, statements, information, opinions, and references ["Content"]. The Content of this book shall not constitute or be construed or deemed to reflect the opinion or expression of the Publisher or Editor. Neither the Publisher nor Editor endorse or approve the Content of this book or guarantee the reliability, accuracy, or completeness of the Content published herein and do not make any representations or warranties of any kind, express or implied, including but not limited to the implied warranties of merchantability, fitness for a particular purpose.

The Publisher and Editor shall not be liable whatsoever...

Made with ❤ on the BookLeaf Publishing Platform
www.bookleafpub.in
www.bookleafpub.com

Dedication

to my younger self, with love.

Preface

Before beginning this journey, I will request you to shed the pretense of pleasing yourself.

Everyone talks about self-love, but nowhere will this book guide you to find your inner self, to become a better version of your own self. Neither is this book a cry for help.

These words of mine, my precious pain painted on the pale screen of your reading device or in the form of a paperback, are about love that got lost in the midst of conversation, at malls and on terraces, amid the loud discussions among our friends, and in the context of what he saw to be duties towards his family.

These are the rage I've tried to suppress and scorch in agony (because I was scared of him more than I was of the world questioning my love). These words of wisdom are a gift left behind in the absence of the love he'd promised me.

This book is a beauty and about everything that you and I have felt but about which neither spoke.

I request you the take the billows in this melancholic ocean as slowly as you can. You won't die in the process. But I assure you that you'll find the self you might've lost in becoming something you're not.

Acknowledgements

This book, a part of me, which you hold now in your precious hands, would not have been possible if jails, my editor, hadn't been part of my life. They are a mentor, a pillar, my constant support, in whom I will always want to confide.

When I started writing, I had always thought in a corner of my mind that I would share my writings and my pain with the world. This was because I'd always been ignored by the person with whom I wanted to share this-- these words which expressed the feeling of neglect, being left out, and taken for granted.

This book, my collection of poems, has wandered among the hearts and minds of my friends and acquaintances. Whenever I was low or wanted to scream, I sought their thoughts and feelings about these poems. So, a big shoutout to them. Without them, I'd never have understood the worth of my words, my pain.

My mother never understood what I recited to her. But at the end of some poems, she would tell me, "I like the tone of this poem". So, a big thank-you to her for always listening to my recitals.

My medicines, without which I don't think I could've got any courage to go through with the publication. I must say, they've immensely helped me to dive into my deeper self and to overcome the fear of being the talk of the show.

Lastly, the people I have loved and were obsessed with.

My Gift of Words

Some gift books
and some materials,
but some memories of love,
of hatred of separation, of meeting.

But a being of words,
I'll gift you
kind sentences, paragraphs,
a story,
an advice when you need,
a walkie-talkie
when your nights get darker.

I promise
I will choose my words-
my breath wisely,
trying not to hurt you
but will be there for you
with the only treasure I have:
of words.

to my beloved, with love

Reincarnation

The fresh air tells me
to write about fresh love—

one that's naive but enthusiastic to learn
(and make mistakes).

In my words,
I will breathe you to understand life,

and be fortunate to live you again,
for a second time.

to my lost lavenders

Fantasy

I can't replace reality
and forever fantasize about
you being beside me.

Your existence is eternal
only in my imagination,

but in truth
you are nowhere to be found.

to my sunflower

Art and Magic

You are no magic
but I am changed,
charmed by your
spells uncast,

the flicking of your brows,
I am jinxed
my true self lost to you!

You, a stranger who creates
this mirage of a flowing brook
in the desert in which I reside,

I am flabbergasted
by the visions of
the universe you take me on tour to–
with your smiles and handshakes!

You tell me I am the art
you never created-
but long to hold by your heart,
tucked under your arms!

So here I am,

having opened myself up,
in museums I've built
out of poems, lines,
words and paintings,
witnessed by the world,

but not by the world
I witnessed in you!

part one

hope

1. Conversation

We share between us, these days,
an uninformed and curious relationship.

The stars and the moon
don't talk much to us
about each other.

But I hope
for a time to come-
when there will be left only:

the stars and the moonlight
for us to talk about.

2. Delusion

I drown myself
in oceans of delusions
when no sounds reach my ears,

my mind shuts out
every thought but yours.

I start reliving memories
which we never made
but I once lived them-
behind closed doors,
amid the crowd,
under the quilt, weeping,
hoping they would become reality.

And with that,
you once again climb into bed.
I lie there, face turned to the wall
and make a sound
as if I've witnessed a ghost.

You talk about what I imagine,
do what I long for,
visit this home,

to leave me deserted.

I, in haste,
not wanting this moment to slip away,
inhale as much of you as I can—
maybe your odour
will be the evidence
that I didn't just imagine things with you,

that you were with me that night,
and some night following that one,
that I've lived a thousand lives through them
in the course of a single breath—

stuck
to the warmth of your skin.

3. Destination

I am not worried about tomorrow,
however it may arrive.

I don't question today,
although it may end bitterly.

With you,
I enjoy every passing second.
I am not stuck,
but heading towards an end
(of many possible ends)
where we will eventually meet (I hope!)

I don't want to define the destination—
to me,
it will be-
a place,
a situation,
a time

where I stop looking for more.

4. The Rotting Apple of my Eye

Words seem worthless when I learn
that the world affects you more than I do.
I paint the sky red
to make the atmosphere lovely,

But you drown yourself in the sea of strangers
and float across the lands of lost lovers.

I feel helpless at your movement
but I still help you reach the edge of the ocean.
And deed done, I dwell
in the dreams of hollow hope—

of admiration returned,
of a return unpromised.

to uplift the love left in loathing
to tell me that I, too, matter
to feed the fountain of famished fondness.

5. Undue

The question is not about what I have
or what I want.

It is about what
you want— forever?
or never?

For you are due to love back
(but I hardly expect
you'd make the payment
till the end).

And the interest
on the unpaid love—
to charge or not to charge?

After all,
it's for love
you never wanted, nor expected

that you're due to repay.

6. Rosebud

I plucked petals from rosebuds,
glitter from dried honey,
and wrote on each of them- 'love'
to send at your doorstep.

In the muffled sounds
of the whizzing moonshine, before dawn,
you must be dreaming of us, maybe?
or of loving someone else forever.

The words on the petals will sound alarm
to wake you up from your dreamland
and bring you to my reality.

The reality of one waiting
with a wail silenced and throttled,
of one who stands to reunite
but is always rebuked for loving too much.

I ignore the world for the world I see in you.
I grow again the seeds of rosy, red love,
I believe in a bunch of thorns
there will still be a bud
which will smile the broadest in my presence.

Thus,
I hope you be a bud,
but a thorn you choose to become.

7. Touch

I want to touch you
at your lips with mine

Dance at the rhythm of my love
with your hip swirling with mine

Jump till our legs hurt
laugh till our cheeks burn

I want to touch your sweat
let it drip and mingle with mine

I want to know
your body more than mine

8. Wanting

I want to
love, love you,
like a crazy madman,
like a wind in rage,
like a lost soul in a maze.

part two

agony

1. A Slap

I am questioning my integrity.

I doubt if I have made adjustments
in love to save something
that was already doomed.

Does a slap have the power
to awaken the soul dying at its hands?

Then why am I still asleep?
I am not abused physically,
maybe I have faced mental manipulation-
unawares.

His falsehood, I assumed
to be an expression of his love—

affection that is
beyond the interpretation
of this generation,
something in which
we both only could converse
and understand.

But when will this stop?
How does it end?

Do I need to stand up to him,
or should I kill my integrity?

And give in to the power of patriarchy.

2. Murder

When I said I am sad,
you told me to smile more often.

I wasn't sure
about the beating of my heart,
you told me
to not pay heed
to the roots of my confusion.

I expressed that
your judgements hurt me unbearably,
you portrayed your statements as
the way to rectify in me-
the wrong and the different.

I told you I think about you
more than necessary,
and you told me not to do so,
as if I were a machine--

all I needed was
to find the controller to switch it off—
my reality.

I told you that I love you,
you said my love is so great
it can't be reached by you.

I remember the day
when I had said to you
that I can't imagine a life without you,

You told me, 'everyone has to die one day'

But don't you remember killing me every day?

3. Pain

Pain persists.
Pain lives within.

It is known now,
for it's my home now.

I understand it, can feel it,
I take it with me everywhere—
this parasite that
lives on my anxieties,
my fears, my thoughts,
on my hollowness.

It is now a friend
which I made when you left.

Unlike you,
it knows how to stay
and never to leave.

4. The Full Halves

I want to rip my pillow into two,
and send the other half to you
and ask you to do the same.

As I've showered
my love, care, wounds,
and loneliness to my half,
You must've done too.

Let's barter these half-pillows
(so much like ripped souls)
join them and let them flow
inbetween—

our thoughts, the half-kiss,
the dreams and memories
and everything it has seen—
our expectations, fears,
the wait, the tears.

Let's stitch our torn selves
and let it share and live
the future we always dreamt
but could never live.

5. The Yin-Yang of Age and Thought

There's no clash
between the age I am in love with
and the thought I drool upon.

But often I wonder
if I am a hard axe upon you:
I gallantly guilt at
my wishful expectations.

I know I have asked you
to be the moon-
where your shine is as warm as the sun.

I talk to you of an age
where loneliness is like
an old friend visiting me,

You fathom my emptiness.
You understand,
the void is because of your absence.

Your understanding of me is accepting.
But there is an ability in your age,

a possibility to expand your vision,
to reach beyond the horizon
and see this absolute wreck.

There are things you do
but there are things I yearn to happen.

Should I blame your age that deters me,
Or be thankful for your consciousness?

6. Nightfall

You were at a distance of
just a touch away,
but I kept myself miles afar.

I had tied a sinful string to you.
Not sure of its naturalness.

Every breath I have exhaled
watching you asleep beside me,
unaware,
has urged me to
feel the feeling I have left unfelt.

'Are you asleep?'
I hoped for sleep to understand
the weight of curiosity upon me.

A million times that night,
I've allowed blood
to flow through veins
and be lost in the lands of confusion.

Do you remember
the hesitant brush of

my fingers upon your skin?

I was scared
to lay the burden of
my loneliness upon you,

and empty you
for the sake of
the void that I bear.

7. A Touch Denied

I fear change.
Not just for me
but for you, too.

The hypothesis of a life
I want to live with you
will dissolve if my thoughts divert.

The years that
I have lived for us,
in the hope of
finding you later,
they will lose their destined meaning.

I measure the happiness
I could be renouncing in the wait—

There might be one, perhaps,
one who would love me.
But there will not be another you.

I dread that
in a year or two
from now, while

we're both breathing,
you might forget
to breathe any love for me?

The present is far from perfect,
but it is with time
that a flower becomes a fruit.
And ripeness becomes its gift.

And in timidity
I live to see if you,
ripe now,
will continue choosing
the blossom over me.

I would not mind it-

if my love for you
were to be shared among others.
But I might lose my mind
if the love—your touch, I so yearn—
were to be shared with others,
(but not with me).

8. Touch II

-a cursing act I perform
on your body consensually,

I assume I am allowed
to cross the carved pretense
between us,

and expose the reality.

I wait to be witnessed,
become the talk of the evening,
for people and for you,
to think-

how mesmerizing I am,
how the movements
of my body
weakens your chain of thought,
and how you are attracted
and unable to think
about anything else but me.

To reach there,
to become an important idea,

I always forget
I need not tell you
about my love,

but leave you wondering
what went wrong,
what was left
to be done-
for me to stay in your life
to love me more
than everyone else.

But then I touch you,
and jinx everything.

part three

promise

1. I Will Stand by You

If you are not at your best on some days,
I will tear off the happiness I carry within
to sit with you in the dark
and cry about life,

I can walk with you
wherever your steps take you,
I will walk by you
so I could shoulder you
if you were to get tired on the way,

I can't bring you the stars, neither count them,
nor can I measure the darkness,

But I have immense happiness
from memories of the time
when you were with me— for me,

Under one roof, sharing your life with me,
laughing your best laugh,
spreading your essence,
eating whatever I had cooked for you,
that's what I have got from you.

I can give it back to you
but I'd also offer you the happiness
I have persevered in the hope—
we will be together, together one day,

Take everything I have
and look at the beautiful life
which I've lived in your company.

At the edge of the bed leaning,
on the pillow sipping the cold coffee
and listening to music, my dear,
'I will stand by you'.

2. You jump, I jump

The world may end tomorrow.
the pandemic, the asteroids
colliding on the Earth,
the melting glaciers
drowning the land of lovers.

These are inevitable.

I will be with you throughout,
I will stick by your shadow silently,
the weather, if it becomes windy,
I will cover your body with my embrace.

If we survive this,
we will sync our steps
on heavy roads.
The coming revolution on Earth,
I will fight along with you.

We humans are the end
to one another, toxic.
Our development and science
is killing innocence.
I promise I will be kind

to help you bloom into a benevolent body.

If the water of the oceans are enraged,
I will be the ship to
sail us to the abode of the heavens.

part four

self-realisation

1. Fight

All I ever wanted was you—
for me to be counted among your own,
to be remembered by you,
to be part of you.

It was always you
who mattered most.

But when you left me,
it was I
who helped myself to keep strong.

Nothing was easy then—
parting parted me,
my heart and my soul.

I faced the unexpected,
I faced myself, dependent,
fighting to be independent,
to be free, to fly, to breathe,
and meet,

one day,
the real me.

2. Selfmade

It was you with whom
I had left my true self,

I was the one with lots of love.

Now, the time has made me fragile.

There is no love left for others,
I am engrossed in loving myself,
finding myself, saving enough love-

-for if someone leaves me,
I must know how to stand still
rather than withering.

3. A New Home

The wait is over now—
It's now us who matters.
Happiness is us.

Empty days are left behind,
never will they come back.

You are home,
let me reach you
and create a place
with our thoughts, love, and care.

It will be a shed for us,
for people who are on the same path-
of love, of togetherness.

4. Holding On

Let us not fall in love
but let love fall
between us.

Everything rushed is wasted.

Love must not be a waste-

it is the purest of
all the elements of nature.

Love for-ever is rare.

Let us be the rarer,
and live forever-
in the arms of each other
holding on to love.

5. The Gasp of Bewilderment

The battle is about living,
death, one day,
will come to me.

Life will take back
every flesh that covers my
sturdy bones,
and offer me the pain to endure,

I will read them as a lullaby
for a somber sleep
to come to me.

I will let life
leave me,

So I can emerge from the whirlwind,
the cyclone, the hailstorm
and the hurricane,
to win.

I need to learn the weakness
before strength burdens me.

I am the art,
I will need time
to be whole,
to make people leave with
the gasp of bewilderment!

6. The Last Song

I am sorry I can't walk anymore.
I am tired,
I have drained myself too much.

I don't know now how to stay alone
when everything has come to an end.
Where I have hoped everything
to end with you.

The shared songs
were left unheard,
my wanting was
marked as the symbol
of detachment foreseen.

I am done.
I am done with wanting more.
I now don't know where to head
and for what to keep moving.

Maybe you will tell me
to live for my own self.
Or for the people
who share the same blood as me.

But do I owe anyone anything?
Even to myself?
I tried to give love my mind desired,
I tried to soothe my body
with the human body and lust on their tongue.

I explained to my lovers how madly I loved them,
I expressed to my father how much I hate him.

No task is left undone,
no people left to please.

I must leave now.
I shouldn't stay more
and be the unwelcomed occupant
on this land of lost lovers.

I am planning to take nothing with me
but hatred for humans.
I want it to be part of my soul,
when I leave my body
I must know
I don't want to become
one of my kind, again.

7. Down The Lane

I will admit
my medicines aren't working on me anymore,
they have failed me,
or those innocents must have
taken the wrong way and body
to dive and settle in?

I am no longer euphoric
no longer as interested as before about life,
chances I am on the wrong drug?

Or high doses
as you said the other day
for my body to cope with it any more
that everything is crashing now?

Did I bring this upon myself?
Is it a duty to feel
to be incompetent
for someone or something
all the time?

What is this sense
of being lost?

Why do I need to be lost first
to find myself later?

Why can't I know
all the answers before
the questions confuse me
and take away my calmness?

Why am I dying
when I should be living!

I am irritated all the time,
I don't know often
how to respond to
unreasonable queries of my mother.

I am worried
if the virus spares me,
What rules must I follow?
Would there be a list of things
a prospectus with
the pieces of information in it
to deal with daily dialects with people?

Will I be able to stay
grounded and not drift away
with the waves of pleasing others

to pass the burden of being left out?

I fear,
even though I consume
stimulants and antidepressants
I fail to believe,
or camouflage the fact
I feel alone--
even in a room full of people.

8. The Devil

The Devil that homes inside me
wears no Prada,
neither it is bothered
to wear anything,
it is naked, shameless.

It walks with me
when I sit at the corner
of the house
revisiting every hurt
which shouldn't be hurting me anymore.

It tells me stories
about stories that lie
in the coffins of the past,
it gives me an insight, a new angle,
a theory to feel more grief
I was feeling it a day ago.

It knows philosophy too,
I guess,
I am not sure,
but it always talks about
how water from the well

is not the rainwater,
but a source that channels
through me to well it up
and fill it to the brim.

Am I the ground, I ask?
It says, 'No, but you are hollow.'

I get confused sometimes
at its replies like this,
but I do wonder
and try to find
the hidden metaphors, if there are any.

At our evening meetings
often it tries to explain to me
how I have sipped
every wretchedness
raining upon me--

with people's worries
I had worried myself,
when they misunderstood me
I have felt
I didn't explain myself enough,
when they said
they can't love me back,

I have stupidly still tried
giving life to a dead corpse,

'These are all,' it says,
sources the well
with my worrying words,
I can drown in it
everything that is hurting.
and end everything
that is overflowing.

9. Mirror

There is a story unrevealed,
in the emotions, the gestures he has lived;
the banarasi saree smells more of him,
struggling to live.

He would go to a friend of his,
his mother's lipstick he would steal,
and paint the reality concealed.
Then an absoluteness he would feel.

Often, he would wear a ghagra,
and witness the transparency of his friend.
It would show the real him;
the one that needed no mending.

He would pretend sometimes
the pain of bearing,
a trauma of womanhood, his femininity,
and then decorate them
on his frugal, pretentious masculinity.

There was a boy who wanted to live,
but his reflection in the mirror outlived him.

10. Lost

Like a clueless fisher in the middle of the sea
I sit fencing my net,
but no lively words come to me to scribble anything.

A chance to be a poet today,
I sense losing it
to the forest fires,
which didn't burn inside me
after the dosage of my wildness.

The flashes of distraction
has slapped me on the face,
the unsolicited images have spanked my brain,
something to nothing was happening to me
but I didn't feel the hit of anything.

I couldn't stop the evening passing by;
perhaps the damage is done,
I have lost my verbosity in the haze.

I see a mountain, a blockage,
its sloppiness seems a bit cluttered,
if I lay my hollowness in the middle of it
might I be able to cross this blunder?

But nothing arouses me;
the moon raises no tides within.
Did I lose my ideas into the periphery
and myself in the vacuum of my own space?

11. One word at a time

I am losing touch,
not detaching,
I mean
I have been swept away.

There is a pandemic
out sprawling on the streets,
and I feel it has
ingested my thinking.

The fantasy poets talk about
through their verses,
I am unable to carve those images.

All I talk about is branches and dead leaves,
maybe sometimes I hide under the moonlight
but nothing more I could think of,

I feel I am a lost cause
or am I being too harsh upon myself?

The smoke of sandalwood burning
never engulfs my surroundings,
the petite pity just hangs

at the edge of my embarrassment,

Do I need to be patient
and feel things
before I assume
I am in pain?

Everything is repetitive,
I am repeating words
and mixing vocabularies over one another.

I am ungrounded,
uprooted like a waste shrub.
My roots are decaying,
and I find no cure for it—

except diving into
the ocean of confusing connotations
and sip in
one word at a time.

12. Un-lost

Like a sand
of hourglass
you slip through my hand
as the cruel time does,

I don't even
feel spent
but you are lost
into the periphery,

I can't gather
the wasted granules
of soil from the land,
but I try to put
your memory into my fist
to remember you
and relish upon your thoughts
a little longer.

I don't know
how far we would
walk together,
I fear for now,
I might lose you

in the darkness of the forest,

Or among the devourers
that starve for you more than I do,

See, I am yet to feel the loss
but as a habit,
I have already started lamenting over it.

13. Wounds

We humans are a house of pains,
someday the fatigue dances on our head
and all we want is to kill
the ache, however possible,

children mostly can't bear
the pulsating pressure at a rotten tooth,
when I was little,
I had always asked my mother
to get rid of the body parts
that hurt me endlessly,

now, the pain that I feel
seems oblivious to many,
when I talk about it,
they laugh at its nonexistence.

I am often told
I need to meditate,
or, move my still muscles
and stand in the postures like saints,
to release the crowded commotion
of my head

it is said, if I follow the absurd rules
I will forget what is hurting
and where it is hurting.

I don't want to lie to myself
everything is okay,
if the buried emotions are breaking me apart
I want to be torn with it.

I don't mind the scars
that will develop after the fight
with the bitter reality,
I can survive wounded
but not dead from the inside.

14. Resistance

Resistance: I feel it surging
over my sad skin,
a force, to put off an alien agitation
that sinks into the pit of my stomach.

This discomfort snatches
my freedom to expose
the excruciating agony,
because in love, I always fail.

I perform no rituals and patterns
to please my beloved,
seldom I bicker about
the bitter taste on my tongue,
I swallow everything
to save myself from nothing harmful.

I tenderly wait for the grey cloud
to be my chaperon to carry the quivering curse
and awake my beloved from the slumber

to tell him I am turning into a corpse
in my breathing body
which is nothing but a sinful snare.

part five

birthing

1. Birth-day

It was dawn, and good riddance for my mother.
The fear of a lily blooming in the verandah was finally over.

Outside, the outstretched blackness was
penetrated with the soft light
of a new day and a new era for my mother.

The blood collected over nine months and nine days
had in its midst an angel trapped in the wrong body.

At the moment of my birth,
the patriarch denied his name
to the blood that ran in the streams of my veins.

No sweets were shared
but the sobs of rejection were the loudest
I was expected to bridge the separated lovers
but it gave him an excuse to shrug me off as a mistake of youth

So, I was celebrated,
with the hope of offering a pillar
to the old age of my maiden mother.

The day I was born,
a coin was tossed in an empty vessel
and the jarring pitch of its reverberation
was thus inscribed on paper.

2. One of a Kind

I can never love myself
until someone loves me
more than me,
More than I have imagined
love to be,
More than it should be,
more than it is allowed.

I will only find solace
in the company of the other,
the one who would want to be lost
in my existence,

would want to breathe
because I breathe,
live because I am alive,
walk because the path
will become beautiful
walking beside me.

Can I wait for someone
to madly fall
in love with me,

Or will I go mad
while waiting to be loved back?

3. Breakthrough

The moment you will
fall in love with me,
I will bury my melancholy peacefully.

Finally, it will be the time you'll see me
beside looking at a skeleton-covered skin.

You'll know who I am,
what I see when I look into your eyes,
how I feel when you choose
my company over others,

You will know even when you'd said
nothing to me or to the air around me
I've hallucinated my name
thousand times in the breeze
coming from you.

You will know I have hoped for a life
in this aimless dancing wind,
I've tried to live-
when the night was unkind
and mornings were rough,

With them, I've made home
I've felt safe
dreaming about you above everyone else.

When you fall in love,
you will eventually know
why was I always ready to drown
even when I knew
how to swim.

4. Reincarnation

I trace the papers end-to-end-
those you have held,
those that were touched by you,

I trace on them-
my hand and fingers,
to imprint my love
on your left presence,

I want to mingle with them,
make a mess of my love
and then throw it into the ocean!

Hopefully, it will sail far away
into the oceans of galaxies
or to the parallel universe.

Maybe there,
I will be allowed
to meet you-
with your hands tugged under mine,
and your kiss on my parched lips.

Maybe I will get a chance

to live with you
and not get strangled
by my miserable
unrequited love.

5. Lend Me a Night

Lend me a night to spend it
sleepless beside you-
only to watch you sleeping,
and stare at you
all through your slipping seconds.

When the harsh morning arrives
to take you from me,
I will look into your eyes-
whom I have witnessed
the night before
taking a peaceful journey
in the lands of lovers,

Those groggy eyes swelled,
and your morning breathe
to sprinkle on me,
your curves and yawns
after the long, tiring trip-

I will take those with me back
to remember you.
How you looked when I had you
while you were lost

in your delusive dream.

Hopefully there,
you might have noticed me-
glancing towards you,
only to make you look back at me.

part six

puberty

1. Serendipity

I was hair-under-my-arms years old
when I accepted the difference in me,
It took my beard and moustache
to tell them not all men wear them
to preach masculinity.

At seven, I was told
the man in our house is not my father,
but a figure to hide
the isolation of a lone woman.

When I first felt the loneliness
brooding in my bonds,
I averted myself from the hurt
which people call destiny, god-written.

I had kin living in the open,
who would scrape my skin in secret.
In the dead of night, he would feel me
in every way I wanted not to be felt.

I took this pity
to garland the pain
that was inflicted in ignorance.

But I was dying in the ashes of
indifference, hate, and name-calling,
just a bag of bones, a hopeless romantic.

I wanted to live, but was made to forget to breathe.

So I blazed to become
the paragon of evolution, and learnt-
that to become a museum
I had to go through the destruction.

part seven

Incompetent

1. Incompetent

What I lack within
to be incompetent
to provide you
the pleasures?

Does my presence
irk the essence
of your being?
Will I become
the embodiment
of hurt for you?

My expression of lust
conjures up to you
only a blatant plead
to suffice my hunger?
Or they tell you
I express because
I am starved.

Should I be damned
before the dusk
settling my life?
Would you not choose

to doom with me?

My stimulants
don't tell me to love you more
with each consumption,
Instead, they help me see
the clearer version
which I denied witnessing
for the namesake love!

I am always last
to reach my beloved
but I am not ridiculed
to arrive leisurely.

Were my absence
obscured by the waves of life
or the weight of friendship?

If I were not
to attain ecstasy with you
why I was aroused
to see the naked soul?

Why am I told
I am the love
that you fear losing

and not the lust
you want to choose?

Over
and over
again.

2. The Next Meeting

Whenever
we meet next,
I will lay
my head
on your lap
or allow yours
to rest on mine.

I will caress your hair
and I will tell you
how I managed
to be apart
for so long,

how I have
struggled to survive,
how on every evening
I have longed
to be hugged,

how I have kept
all my love safely
in my heart
for you

to sip on
whenever we
meet next.

2. Dawning

Weights, iPad and cats
they are close to me,
sat, ideally, untouched
and ignored.

The cats had the food
just a while ago,
but maybe they need water?
I should place a bowl of it.

No, I am not able to do it.

I can't remember
where I last put my charger,
Is it left in your bag?
I hope not.
No, I don't want to walk down
the same lane again
where you will be at the end.
Anymore.

No, I should manage without it,
I will just borrow it from a friend nearby.
Yes, that will help me to cope for a while.

Weights, urgh, exercise!
How much humans are expected to exert
until they are exhausted from living!?

What weight should I carry today?
Maybe a little less than the weight of surviving.
I will skip adding the slide of anxiety
to my dumbbells today,
and perhaps a less heavy depression would do?

It is past the sunlight now,
the dusk is almost leaving from here,
twilight, I think I will spend it
thinking about you.

I need not waste my time now,
I should go back to the absurd normal
where you don't exist anymore.

Or can I just sit here
in front of the alien screen,
where I am on some website
trying to figure out
where do I go wrong
when it comes to expressing!

And as I am typing words,
phrases or angry sentences
about your actions.
everything is underlined with red,
this site is suggesting me
to rephrase my feelings.

Sigh.

4. An Ode to A Journey

I write so I can weep through words.
I don't dare to go to people
and tell them they affect me.

To weave emotions with wonderment
wasn't planned or foreseen.

Out of the blue,
the evening I had written
about the pain of separation,
you had exclaimed surprise at
how I could relate to something not experienced.
In return, I had asked you where you belonged.

'In the arms of a loving woman',
you had said.

I learnt that night
I could resurrect my feelings
massacred at your hands
and let them die again
with wilting vocabularies.

The destroyers aren't the same now, but

I still create the mirage in poetry
and painful odes of the world I couldn't live in.

5. The Wisdom of Wilting

I am the words that
my mind failed to vocalise.

Mistakes are friends.
They help me be
on the path of evolution.

I wear eccentricity as the only cloth—
It reveals my vulnerabilities.

Education, for me, is
a means to make a living

But words are wagons—
they take me to places
where, with the wisdom of wilting,
I create another place.

I love watching
the beauty of nature,
the art of artists,
the face of my beloved.
These creations soothe me.

The idea of painting showed me
there is more to living.

Sketching, a surprise.
I sketch the person
I love the most,
and realise that he lives
through and through me.

Few people matter to me.
I am not a loud one.
My silence is the armour
that protects me from
unwanted beings around.

Making conversation through
letters, emails, or chats,
I try to reconnect with the lost lavender.

I write because
the emotions I hold for him
couldn't be expressed in gestures and voices.

So, I let them dance on paper.

With me breathing my last,
 my words will come to a halt.

But they will keep travelling
to attain eternity.

Postface

You have read the book, all the poems. You have lived a life, you have felt things. You have become something with every word that was written. I am proud of you. I am happy for your heart. I am happy that you became a poem with me in the process. I am happy for your new life after this book.

Everything that I have written here has come from a place of hurt, healing, and living. I have loved people, and I believe I will keep loving people until the end of time. It will mean I will get hurt many times, but without hurting, are we even living?

Thank you for becoming part of my life.

While in COVID, everything was difficult, sitting idle at home made me feel many things, from leaving to living, I have come far. Initially, being a part of another publishing house, this book has touched many hearts. With BookLeaf Publishing, I wish to reach many hearts, too. The reason to discontinue with them and set this book freshly again with BLP for readers is something important. I do not want to say much, but every life matters; that is what I believe. That's it. Thank you.

Also from Author

bachpan and baddua

www.ingramcontent.com/pod-product-compliance
Lightning Source LLC
Chambersburg PA
CBHW060203050426
42446CB00013B/2977